A Collection of Chaos

A
COLLECTION
of
Chaos

A poetic recollection of pain, lost love,
apocolyptic visions, and authentic
communication with the dead.

Christine Chaos

iUniverse, Inc.
New York   Bloomington

A COLLECTION OF CHAOS
A poetic recollection of pain, lost love, apocolyptic visions, and authentic communication with the dead.

iUniverse books may be ordered through booksellers or by contacting:

iUniverse
1663 Liberty Drive
Bloomington, IN 47403
www.iuniverse.com
1-800-Authors (1-800-288-4677)

Because of the dynamic nature of the Internet, any Web addresses or links contained in this book may have changed since publication and may no longer be valid. The views expressed in this work are solely those of the author and do not necessarily reflect the views of the publisher, and the publisher hereby disclaims any responsibility for them.

ISBN: 978-1-4502-5714-5 (sc)
ISBN: 978-1-4502-5715-2 (ebk)

Printed in the United States of America

iUniverse rev. date: 09/20/2010

I DEDICATE THIS BOOK TO THE LIVING GOD
WHO GUIDES AND WORKS THROUGH ME
AND TO MY LOVING FAMILY
THANK YOU

Table of Contents

JILL OF ALL TRADES

Jill of all trades, master of some
Prepare for my moment to serve with the Son

All things to all people, but serve God alone
At home in all places, but longing for Home

We speak very often, you'd be quite surprised
He'd speak to you too, if you'd open your eyes

Suffering tells stories; I've got quite a few
Life's learn-ed lessons, can't get in a pew

Men in my life, draw in close, fall in love
Don't seem to realize, all charms from above

I'm lured to darkness, to let in the Light
Shadows reach for me, in fear of their plight

Dead or alive, their souls feel life's pain
My heart hears the cries, my soul feels the same

SMALL TALK (an Introduction to the World of Chaos)

For me, it is much easier to create lyrical poetry that delves into my deepest, darkest past, than it is to talk small. My words are raw and unpolished, but I like it that way. "Nice weather we're having.", "How was your weekend?", "Do you have a dog or a cat?", "A house or a flat?" BLAH, BLAH, BLAH.

To memorize and recite Shakespearian prose in front of thousands is a treasure. But, to waste words and energy on such meaningless dribble, that's an atrocity! What are your thoughts, what of your dreams? Yes, I actually do care! Forget politeness, political correctness, introduce me to your other side, you know, the one you have to hide. For me, I wish I could hide the 'Christine light' side. It's a mask that comes out in church, in public places, or talking to a colleague that I can barely stand. Don't show your feelings, don't tell the truth, keep your emotions consciously aloof.

But small talk means so much to some people, and that's when it matters. It matters to the quiet man who obviously has been painfully shy his whole life. It matters to the awkward girl who everyone picks on behind her back. If I had a dime, for every guy who fell for me, simply because I took the time to make small talk when no one else would, I'd have a lot of dimes. So you may ask, "why would someone who cares so much about honesty, lie about her identity?" Well, I poetically embellish real events I have witnessed in my lifetime, because I feel most people out there can relate. But if the people who have inspired me found out just how transparent they really are, they'd be crushed. I would never want to hurt anyone's pride just to dig deeper into their hearts and souls and to seek "poetic justice" for the pain found there. I have also found that most people, who do deliberately hurt others, have mastered this technique as a defense mechanism to hide their own insecurity. A kind word can go a long way with this type.

Every opportunity I have in life to tell the truth, and not get fired, I do it. This habit has taken me far in life, for it's what is unexpected. Telling the truth has the ability to make you stand out in a crowd and disarm the defensive. I once had the most interesting conversation with a wrong number simply because he knew we'd never meet. I never did get a name, what a shame.

Why are we so afraid of honesty? There are some truths to avoid, if they are unnecessary, and they will only lead to pain. To hurt someone for no reason is uncomplimentary to your own being. If you take a sincere interest in what makes someone 'tick', you can be a friend to one who normally makes you sick. They might surprise you.

SHINE THE LIGHT- THOU SHALL NOT LIE

Why do I feel it is necessary for most of my poems to rhyme? I think some words and ideas in a collegiate style poem, come off as pretentious to the average person. I'm not looking to be overly deep or to please the critics. I want to touch the common heart and entertain with truth. For those who wish to stand up in front of throngs of people, pretending to be more intellectual than they are, I say "get a life". I just want people to know that they are not alone. We all hurt, we all can see the pain in others and feel helpless, but there is someone looking after us, loving us, especially when we feel most unloved. Whatever name you want to give it, there IS a bigger picture, a master plan, and you are worth far more than some monkey on a tree.

There is beauty in simplicity. You don't need a college degree or high IQ to understand it. Just open your heart, listen to the words, and think of them as lyrics to a tune only you know. Personally, I'm not into poetry, unless it really tries to find that hidden place in my soul. So if I can manage to entertain you, and make you feel understood at the same time, than I've done the job I set out to do. Please enjoy, I hope you do. I'm not smarter or better than anybody else, God just allows me the gift of empathy, and the ability to see something others cannot or chose not, to see.

Yes, I've seen many souls. I have been able to see them since I was seven. Mom quite often found out through research, that many of my invisible friends had been alive at one time. The problem with believing in a Creator or in ghosts is that we as humans try to understand it logically with our own perception of time and space. Do you think that is how the universe sees us? Souls are in an entirely different plane than we are; time is irrelevant to nature, as it should be. I know the truth, the gift for what it is. But it is important to me to tell others so that they understand, and hopefully believe, that there is a part of us that cannot be seen with the naked eye. The soul is eternal, and we might want to consider setting up a nice retirement home that doesn't require a large savings account. How you do that is up to you, I don't have all the answers. I just want to encourage you to give it some thought, and bring to light that which others chose to hide. I hope and pray that in some small way I am able to help you.

Sincerely, Christine Chaos

VISION IN THE DARKNESS

Darkness engulfs me, swallows me whole
Burning fires, in my zealous soul
Light my way, and take control

Tangible, momentous, these must be
All these visions that I see
Consuming me, so violently

Lust for dusk, to usher the Light
Sorrow, mourning, for their plight
"Lord this is an endless night!"

All these ghosts surround me so
Tingling, reaching, can't let go
So much more, have yet to grow

Let me know Thy master plan
Let me know just where I stand
Lead me forward, guide my hand

Too much knowledge, I cannot handle
"Mock me, and I'll dust my sandals"
Bible rests upon my mantel

My false pride, my own distraction
Put on face, perform the action
Never for worldly satisfaction

Eyes so tired, need to rest
With this Bible, upon my chest
My worn heart, consumes my breast

Lonely, sadness, visions vivid
Calling, grasping, spirits livid

Eyes closed shut, but still I see
Faces, arms, that reach for me

"Help me Lord, away please send!"
Was so weak, prayed gift to end

Blank, vacant stare and no reflection
"Forgive me Lord, for my rejection."

On the floor, and now I'm kneeling
"My gift return!" Pray for the healing

Longing now, my soul returned
One more lesson, I have learned

Gazing glass, what do I see?
At last my soul, returned to me

"Oh, so grateful for this gift!"
"Teach me now, your souls to lift!"

"She's so crazy, she's a liar!"
Soon will witness, my soul's fire

DEATH DOES NOT BECOME HER

She appears from the shadows, tear drop in her eye
Thought her pain would end quickly, but was sold a lie

She reaches out, to reveal her split wrists
Silently questions, "What fate this black twist?"

Cutting, slicing, over and again
Bleeding, purging, but never to end

Lips are blue, pale the skin
Eyes of black, the darkest sin

The greatest gift from Lord above
You in His image, His total love

But you rejected, tried to send back
Into His face gifted, the hardest slap

Life was "too hard" to endure 'til end
But did you ask help, from God or a friend?

Now you suffer and know REAL pain
Feeling the knife, again and again

Blade to flesh and what's your gain
Now forever your blood will stain

I do not know how hard was your life
But now I see an eternity of strife

You gather before me, in condition's last throws
What led to this place? Only you can know

Your suffering on Earth, could continue relentless
For your sin now repenting, plead His forgiveness

There is no relief from your chosen dark sight
No human can help, lead you into the light

What's done is done, deed committed in haste
To walk in your nightmare, life a sacrificed waste

I wish I could save you, my heart is now breaking
You're cold, you're alone; you're trembling and shaking

Your lips are moving, I'm afraid I can't hear you
Your regret's so evident, but your grief can't subdue

Your hair is dark as your eyes will remain
Your soul will bleed on and your flesh does the same

You hold in your hand, the weapon of choice
Continue to plead with sad lips and no voice

Now I must leave, not completing my task
I will pray for your soul, for salvation I'll ask

INVISIBLE

I'm invisible to all who see
But not to her, she smiled at me

She's not to know, how much that meant
For with this act, I'm heaven sent

They all taunt and put me down
So worthless; Nothing; Nature's clown

But she defends, asks how I feel
How can I show her, love is real?

My whole world here remains in sadness
Her face appears, my heart felt gladness

Today she asked me for my name
Oh, maybe her heart feels the same

So beautiful and popular
To all who know her, she's a star

I build my courage, force my might,
Everyday she fills my sight

They mock me, spit, and stomp my pride
From all but her, my soul, I'll hide

She's reading the same book as I
All I feel, can't be a lie

She's with her friends, he's kissing her
All my rage and hate does stir

Why must I always be alone?
Why can't I fight him, claim his throne?

My face is scarred, so cruel the mirror
My life so far, so full of fear

For five full minutes, today we talked
In front of *them,* together walked

Now my thoughts grow thick and smother
To my worlds end, I'll love no other

In my dreams, I lie with her
A flood of feelings, my body stirs

No other girl, gave time of day
All my emotions, compelled to say

Tomorrow's fate, I'll take my stand
Heart sacrificed, to hold her hand

All night long, I plot and scheme,
Poetic words, to share my dreams

She's a mirage, across the room
Dream of the day, I'd be her groom

Fail to get her, all alone
Perhaps tonight, I'll try the phone

I look her up, I hear her voice
So hard to speak, is *this* my choice?

Finally now, my courage gathers
Face to face, I'd so much rather

She's not sure, just who I am
I remind her. Makes me a man

My mouth bleeds words, so vulnerable
Comprehend her answer? I'm not able

"I'm so flattered, I really am"
"But you see, I have a man"

My heart is shattered, the pain severe
My tortured future, becomes so clear

Her niceties spoke all with pity
Wish I could run, just leave this city

THE SICKNESS

It starts cold, deep within my core
Body remembers, brain does no more
A sickness lingers, without a sore
Wait for the Lord to settle the score

Invisible scars that never will heal
What horror did little panties reveal?
A violation far too real
Unworthy trust, innocence did steal

It happened to me, it happened to you
How many get caught? Far too few
His lust made sick, what his heart did rue
Some won't touch, some just view

The only answer left to heal me
Forgiveness without an apology
He'd never admit to himself or Thee
But God forgives what's dark in me

A childhood lost, was his only power
In this sickly, forbidden hour
I feel my weakness in the shower
Lord can help, make new the flower

Far too common, we will weep
Behind dark corners, they do creep
Through soiled windows, they do peep
What they have sewn, they SHALL reap

WRATH

HYPOCRITES IN EVERY PEW
CHRISTIANS HERE? SO VERY FEW
MAKE MY RAGE AND VENOM SPEW

HOUSE OF GOD OR DEN OF THIEVES?
DEPENDS ON WHO YOU CAN BELIEVE
FOR THEIR OWN GAIN, THEY WILL DECEIVE

JUDGEMENT BLOCKING EVERY THOUGHT
CHILDREN FORGET WHAT THEY WERE TAUGHT
MOCK THE LEADER, DON'T GET CAUGHT

PARENTS COME FOR TRADITION'S SAKE
NOT ONE EFFORT DO THEY MAKE
WORSE THAN AGNOSTIC, TO BE FAKE

PROTESTANT, LUTHERAN, ROMAN CATHOLIC
FALSE THE IDOLS, MAKES ME SICK
GOD'S WRATH GROWS AND TIME DOES TICK

SO I'LL MAKE MY CHURCH AT HOME
WORKPLACE, WOODS, CREEKS THAT FOAM
FOR I'LL FEEL HIM MORE IF I'M **ALONE**

THE DARK FOREST, THE ELEMENTAL

Driving on a country road, beauty all around...
Suddenly the sky grows dark, with its sense, I'm found

Created by men and their demon, vengeance was its purpose
Its age to me remains unknown, dark history will surface

It cannot hurt, nor make me fear, for my Lord is always near

But as I pass it watches me, very slowly through the trees

The land was stolen, pillaged such; the natives here were crushed too much

Gathering to chant and sing; butchered, made this horrible thing

Not quite man and not quite beast; revenge and justice is unleashed

Man cannot destroy or tame, so in the woods it will remain

This one's old, I cannot see, but know with soul, it's watching me

Once before I saw its kind, man above and beast its hind

Charging from the woods towards me, eyes glare red, it turned to flee

A physical being it was true, my friend was there, he saw it too

I swear its legs with feathers covered, no soul to see, its life force smothered

What evil created this dark art? To this day my brain does smart

Once a thing like this brought near, take a warning, hard and clear

'Tis not natural to in darkness play, beckon spirits, as tribes may

Vengeance in haste towards another you hate
YOU CANNOT DESTROY, WHAT YOU DID CREATE

ALONE

Alone I walk, I know this place
Though I cannot make out the time or space

I know that I've been here before
That's all I know, recall no more

The dark and cold surrounds me so
But the pain is gone, where did blood go

I was here, and he was there
A gun went off, still feel his stare

Far away I see a light
Fear holds me from visiting that sight

I will retreat, I'll go back home
Already here, and so alone

The day's begun all over again
Failure- tried to call my friend

The dog he sees me, knows I'm here
What's going on, it's so unclear

I shout, I scream, no one replies
And now my fear I cannot hide

I wait for such and endless time
I hear a name, it sounds like mine

Who are these people in my home?
Now I wish I was alone

One can see me, reaches out
"Leave me alone!" I want to shout

She tells me in the light, there's hope
A way to truth, a way to cope

I just don't know who I should trust
But communicate with her I must

She's crying now, she feels my pain
I'm bleeding now, I feel the same

Again, I'm on the road alone
But, now reach for the light I'm shown

No more confusion, no more pain
No more hurt and no more shame

Forgiveness here, the way is clear
My loved ones shine and draw in near

THE X

Divorce papers were quickly signed.
Trying to create a clever rhyme
Why should I waste my precious time?

With you, I wasted time enough
Dealing with all your wicked stuff
Does hitting women, make you tough?

Vicious words sting worse than fists
Throw a beer can, grab my wrists
Magnificent dream, what nightmare this?

Once to bed, to this day I rue
Without the violence, couldn't see it through
Was I the monster, or was it you?

Now I see you, half erect
Not enough rage, I do suspect
So many issues, I can detect

A marriage should not have a boss
No heartache here and no love lost
Hard to believe, at such a cost

But, really dear, I must thank you,
For showing me, what *not* to do
For now I know my love is true

You've found your mate, and so have I
Praise God above, live not a lie
New love will last, 'til the day we die

The ugly side brought out of me, the true face out on you
I thought I knew you oh so well, you proved I never knew

THE BLIND

**Those who see with just their eyes, would be better off without them,
For maybe then they'd see the light, of hearts and souls around them.**

How they look with hearts closed tight,
Judging hard with all their might!

"Look at her, that big, fat slob"
"Get off your ass, and get a job"

Just don't care, what pain she's in,
Blind to just how much they sin.

"My beautiful house, my shiny car."
"My perfect kid, the super star."

No time to give, no time to help;
Hoarding up their "hard earned" wealth.

Absurd to walk another's mile,
That burden might just crack their smile.

Responsible, practical, patriotic, polite;
When the end is near, I pity their plight!

Their good deeds done with show and flare,
But only when there's time to spare.

They're empathetic to no one,
Go to church, but know no Son.

To understand another's life,
One must know the pain and strife.

You give with all the "widow's might",
But don't save money, "that's just not right!"

Someday they'll know just whom they've hurt, and suffer with that truth,
For they were judging God Himself, and they *will* have their proof!

FOREVER FIGHT

I'm fighting them, they're fighting me
Trying so hard just to make them see

Fact is fiction, fiction fact
We have no proof, perform the act

They won't believe, without their "proof"
Why does God stay so aloof?

To see God, "faith" is no more
Devil would win, he's keeping score

Logic can only make more tragic
Comparing faith to believing in magic

The battle wages on; we fight
But losing soldiers from the light

They tire quickly, lose faith and hope
Our numbers dwindle, but still we cope

However long it takes my Lord
My armors plated, truth my sword

Your reasoning, I know not yet
But You are wise, Your time is set

When the truth, at last revealed
The wicked will know, their fate is sealed

The darkening sun, the moon as blood
The great destruction, worse than the flood

Then all will see, and all will know
Their choices made, their blood will flow

And souls will witness, Hell on Earth
You made your choice, here comes your curse

Until the Lord comes back around
I'll steel myself, and hold my ground

Well you know what it's like, I don't got to tell you
Who puts up a fight, walking out of hell now

The White Stripes, "I fought Piranhas"

WITHDRAWAL

This sickness, a million tiny deaths
But no morbid escape
The weakness spreads
Living, giving water oozes from every cell in my body
That no liquid can quench
Longing great pain to distract from the tedious,
Suffocating imbalance
Cannot rest, cannot heal. Miniscule pain so very real
Doomed to suffer mediocrity
Craving an end to this unreal reality
No food to touch my tongue
For fear of the violent return
No wisdom to escape the reach of the Reaper
No, not death, no such freedom
These unspeakable nightmares, arrive without sleep
Possible to see the future, but no strength to defend against it
Turn to the Savior for strength
My own being involuntarily rejects that comfort
Though mind and soul want nothing else
Spread like wildfire, under protection of invisibility
These monotonous tiny diseases
Once and again will be the center stage
During this insufferable drought

BEWARE THE CONCEALED FACE

Treachery, malice, cunning, deceit
Your crocodile tears fall hard at my feet
Your verbal venom, so sickly sweet

The trick of your tongue, taunts us to confide
Unaware of your stripes, your true other side
A Christian breastplate, the Lord must provide

Behind glowing smile, you've hidden your sneer
Choosing which victim's name to smear
Until it's too late, your intention's unclear

A friend to all whom remain so lost
A wing to wrap under, warm and soft
Don't mind the sword, the hidden cost

A pat on the back, where knife can be placed
Life caused you such pain, conceal leather with lace
What turned you to predator, your new second face?

MY FOREVER LOVE

Another life, another time
Our souls were one, lives intertwined

Is this our fourth, fifth time around?
Last time I searched, not to be found

Now here you are, but I'm too late
I leave alone, my heart to fate

The years will pass, with last breath's end
We'll meet again, don't forget, my friend

Our souls in cycle, all through the years
Heart's open wound, my soul in tears

Our eyes will meet, as strangers pass
Remember your embrace, of our time last

It will meet completion, on His returning
Unite us again, and end this yearning

My soul mate true, what have we done?
That we must wait, 'til breaking Son

THE RED COAT

Heading out, starting my hike
My body reacts, heightened my psyche

Before I see him, I feel his presence
A constant reminder, of my six senses

And here I happen, upon "his" trail
Breeze in the trees, enhanced to a gale

His eyes; no eyelids, a deep, piercing stare
To this day can't escape, his dream haunting glare

Upon a partial stallion, it's clear
Legs and snout fail to appear

He will not approach or communicate,
For his heart is full of rage and hate

No prisoners of war, would be set free
Torture and rape, fills his heart with glee

The Native girls would be his treasure
A soldier's suffering, would bring him pleasure

A hundred years, he still rides here
No help from me, would come, so clear

I am surrounded by a permanent light
He was drawn over, a curious sight

With me he could never touch or harm
But "get off *his* path", would be my alarm

For a moment only, his soul I did see
But his gaze remains, for a lifetime with me

HEAVENLY HOST

Our innocence ends when we see them no more
Toddlers and pets still witness the score

When we are lost, in our darkest hour...
They arrive to console, yet we are too sour

We don't believe, what we still cannot see
But, when we were babies, of course we believed

Now our eyes are clouded such...
That to witness them, would be too much

My "Fat Charlie", how I miss you
With me through a childhood, one couldn't construe

I know you're still here, always at my side
So, why then Sweet Charlie, continue to hide?

The unspoken law, the dead I can see
But angels must wait, until they set me free

THE WARNING

This old house, what secrets keep?
Pipes cry out, floors do creak
Objects move, did someone speak?
I wish that I could get some sleep!

"Get up quickly, write this down!"
Fire, chemicals, cities drown
Tornadoes, earthquakes, shake the ground
"A different story, when I'm back around!"

Now I see a man's wife dying
Don't understand, 'til he's really crying
"Come on girl, just keep on trying!"
"What do you think, your dreams are lying?"

Witness the souls, they cannot see
This little girl just wants her mommy
Cry for this one, set her free
Now that they know, at rest can be

"I've shown you much, and you believe"
Proof and facts, all they perceive
"Get them in step, or without them leave"
"Times running out, I don't deceive"

Observe the shadow, feel his pain
All his days run out in rain
Stuck here always, until I came
Now for him, it's not the same

"This is MY power, don't you forget!"
"You take the credit, and you'll regret!"
So many more souls to help yet
"They don't listen, don't you sweat!"

I feel the hurt, I hear their sighs
They're all around, you don't realize
"My child dear, release their cries"
"Touch their souls, open their eyes"

Others still within their body
Selfish, cruel, sometimes just naughty
Throw some fists, when they feel rowdy
Destructive course, to remain so bawdy

Don't understand what you can't perceive
Showed me once, I still believe
"In this world, you work for ME"
"My time's at hand, diminishing eve"

A candle that burns twice as bright
"I gave you wisdom, gave you sight"
"These gifts you have, don't take light"
"I'm coming soon, could be tonight!"

THE FOREST OF AZURE

Alone in the woods, I sense they are close
The Father, the Son, and the Holiest of Ghosts

Look to the canopy, life in the leaves
Like little hands, they wave in the breeze

Watch as the sunbeams, stream down through the clouds
They, like God's fingers, are a contact allowed

Every tiny miracle, brings me to wonder
The sun and the rain, the lightning and thunder

Every little being, is quite necessary
Food for the critters, not meant to be scary

From the tedious mosquito, to the black bear whose roaring
The birds in the air, the majestic eagle soaring

Oh what a privilege, is just to notice
Yet God uses it all, to get to know us

Goosebumps on flesh, out in His forest
My own private church, the Host sings the chorus

All wonderful noises, creeks and animals making
All this is for us, ours free for the taking

Thank you so much, for Your beauty abounds
Brings delightful peace, down here on Your grounds

PRAYING TO BLEED

I welcome the silence, for it comes not with pain
Nor worry, nor anger, nor experience to explain

We commune without words, for they are just so fleeting
Our everyday burdens, with rain, come off sheeting

It drums in my ear, no suspense and no fear
He stares straight ahead, does he think of me near?
Would I sense nothingness; will I hold back a tear?

The rain it beats down on the glass so protective
What of us inside, unspoken thoughts so collective
Not boredom, it's true, not routine, but not pensive
Just peace here inside; no, my heart's not expensive

Most find us quite lacking, they need their distractions
To cover what's missing in their own satisfactions

For me love is quiet; true, words are so needless
I will cherish the silence, but pray womb remains seedless

I am late, but avoid the possibilities that meaning
For three is a crowd, and I'm definitely not beaming
But not with a murderous heart am I scheming

I know his love would go on until dying
But if life were truth, to myself I'd be lying
When we entered this contract, only two would be signing
A third be a burden, break our life without trying

I cherish each moment as though it were last
This love incomprehensible, much more than my past

I'll live here in this silence, and peace I'll be keeping
Pray for merciful blood, to avoid that harsh speaking

ACT 4, SCENE 3

SET: Medieval torture chamber/dungeon. Various torture devises. Leather masked muscular man is holding a whip; a guard is standing next to the prisoner, our heroin, who is shackled, faced towards a stone wall....

Our lady, with long, strawberry blond, wavy hair, is dressed in expensive velvet, period dress. She is quietly praying as she awaits punishment. Torture master is staring straight ahead, awaiting instruction. The Bishop enters, proudly...

Guard: "Why did you choose this course for yourself? As a lady of the Queen, your life was good, was it not?"

Lady: "It was chosen *for* me, and it is far more important to have a good eternal life."

The Guard sighs deeply, then storms out, disrespectfully ignores the Bishop. He loves her, and knows there is nothing he can do to prevent the suffering that lays ahead for her; without risking his own life.

Bishop: "So, you thought you could defy God and the Holy Catholic Church. Your insubordination is spreading like a disease! What say you for your evil deeds?"

Lady: "*You* are the Beast that defies my God!"

Bishop: "The Church *is* God!"

Lady: "No, the church thinks it is more important than the word of God! It lies and steals from the Lord's true people, to feed its own lust for wealth and power. You commit the most atrocious forms of blasphemy with your own venomous tongue!

Bishop: "You are a witch, and you will die a most horrible death, and your soul will burn for an eternity in the fires of Hell!"

Lady: "It is your own soul you should concern yourself with. You twist the sacred words to serve your own selfish needs. You do Satan's own bidding and you will suffer for it until the end of time."

Bishop: "How *dare* you speak such lies to me!!"

Lady: "How dare *you* steal from the poor to feed the wealthy?! How dare *you* plunder and pillage, murder and rape in the name of our Lord to serve your own good!?! Mark my words, God will show you NO mercy, as according to what you have shown so many of His children!"

Bishop: "You FILTH! I have done no such things!"

Lady: "You have done far worse, because you demand others administer your evil will on your behalf, so that they too will have to suffer for your sins. For this reason, your punishment will be ten times greater than theirs combined!"

Bishop (shouting): "NO ONE WILL SUFFER AS GREATLY AS YOU WILL NOW!!"

Lady: "I fight for the Lords justice, nothing you do can hurt me, for my soul is eternal and my body is mortal! One day the people will rise against your corruption and tyranny!"

Bishop: "The people are fools; they will do what I say, especially after they hear of your fate! (to Torturer) Make her pain and weeping legendary!!"

Lady: "Only Christ's suffering was legendary, 'When you do unto the least of these, you do unto me'."

Bishop: "What did you SAY?! You dare take the Holy text and use it for your blasphemy!?"

Lady: "No, I use Christ's words to drive out the demon in you!"

To Torturer; Bishop: "Beat her as though your life depended on it!!"

He starts to walk briskly toward the door. Waits and smiles as he hears her dress torn to reveal her back. The whip is raised as she prays quietly. Then her body goes limp.

Bishop: "You fool! What are you waiting for!?"

Torturer: "Your Holiness, she has fainted."

Bishop: "Nonsense, it's a trick!"

He storms over to her, "Wake up you whore!" He goes to slap her, and then stops.

Bishop: Quietly; "She hasn't fainted, she's dead."

The torturer drops his whip, takes off his mask, drops to his knees and begins praying. Bishop is silent, dumbfounded.

CURTAIN

THE NURSE

The windows are boarded, save but a few
With menacing shadows, an ominous hew

And from the same shadow, her long golden hair
She's waving and crying, beckoning me there

So limited and helpless, can't think of a line,
To let me gain entry, past no trespassing sign

Each day that I pass her, heart melts at her plea
To help heal the injured, she's calling to me

A sea, a mirage of unending pain
Her field as a healer, would always remain

If I could find out, this hospital's history...
No stories or websites, to help solve the mystery

Its doors were closed in decades past
But for her, memories of agonies last

To enter the building, for me as a stranger,
Vagrants and hoodlums and structure a danger

I'm at my wits end, my hands remain tied
Can't escort her soul, to the other side

What can I do for a soul such as this?
What is the clue that my own soul has missed?

So for the time being, I'll continue to pray
Until passage is open, and Light finds a way

THE NICE GUY

I was ten and she was two, a "little pain", but then she grew

Confusing feelings, hormones bound, as we wrestle, on the ground

Throw the ball; go for a ride; never to be satisfied

Her love and kindness make me shudder; looks upon me, as a "brother"

Watch her grow, watch her learn, watch my heart forever yearn

Athletic, pretty, and so clever; to hold my hand though; no, not ever

Fourteen now and side by side, love too strong to try to hide

Not the same; father, mother, but she sees me, as her "brother"

Try to tease her as a sister, my pain oozes like a blister

Sixteen now, opens the flower; why does *he* have all the power

Her brother's friend, I do remain; part of family, I became

Worse this fear than any other, will I always be her "brother"?

My parent's love was so unclear, unconditional is this family here

Women in this world so cruel, so my soul, she's bound to rule

She tries hard, not to hurt me; but my heart is crueler than she

Have a sister, need a lover, but for her, remain a "brother"

Twenty now, watch her glow; my loves so real, she *has* to know

So strong for me, she needs to flee; oh, this pain is **killing** me

My mind is like an open book, she dodges fast, avoids the hook

Easier not to have a lover, my love sees me as a "brother"

She sees through me, has to be, "you're always such a *friend* to me"

Saw her everyday it seemed, but now she's busy, chasing "dreams"

Soft her words, worse than rejection; looks to me just for protection

She's forever with another, ALWAYS to remain her "brother"

THE BLACK SEED

The black, evil seed is following me,
I'm running on razor thin wire.
Nothing but open air beneath me,
The sky above is fire.

So tiny I barely see it,
But the threat is oh, so real.
If it succeeds in catching up with me,
My tomb of anguish sealed.

What keeps me on my toes,
While my feet are slowly bleeding?
Out of breath, end of my rope,
The pain intense, it's seething.

Running forward to light so bright,
My goal so far away.
Angel's wings must keep me up,
For, I never fall or sway.

The light is God, the black is Satan,
The dream, it keeps repeating.
But beyond this chase, it seems to me,
I cannot catch it's meaning.

I dreamt it first, when I was small,
Terror of my own construction.
I know without the aid of God,
My end would be destruction.

Yet the dream, it comes again,
Sometimes when I'm awake.
There must be more importance here,
In my brain's dark, abysmal quake.

So simple is this game of life,
And yet so complicated;
If You indulge me understanding,
I would surely be elated!

LEARN FROM THE DINOSAURS

Science and theology, agree it **will** end
It will be much sooner than you're thinking my friend

Ponder the dinosaurs and their great demise
What can we learn from the weak and the wise?

Christians believe, "like a thief in the night"
Society says different, but both may be right

Beyond all the earthquakes, floods, and great fires…
Suffocation, flesh melting, souls revealed as great liars

There will come a time and we'll need to be ready
Is your soul prepared, or is your heart still quite heavy?

Witnessed in visions, creates fire in my mind
The destruction and terror, I've seen all the signs

"Not in my lifetime", we cry in denial
But this life's illusions may confuse and beguile

From the beginning, predictions were made
The great flood **did** happen, how many were saved?

Will we learn from the past or continually delude?
The nightmares I've seen, prophets have construed

The details are sketchy, not meant to be known
Mass destruction of past, fact that science has shown

No one can prevent, what **will** come to pass
Just remember the soul, will the body outlast

Cannot put into words, the torments I've seen
Witnessed since childhood, awake and in dreams

Many small visions, already completed
My lack of understanding leaves fate undefeated

I stake my life on it, all **will** be revealed
The time is at hand, death's secrets unsealed

Prepare and believe, the choice yours alone
Remember it's too late, when at last truth is shown

PAIN

All consuming and irrational
Continuous, never ending, tedious; **torture**

Pray to stay sane
Cope
No choice, just cope

"Could be so much worse, could be paralyzed"

"We can't help you", "take this", "swallow that"
Cope
Sleepwalk through endless days with no amount of rest enough to satiate

Sleepwalk; a living, breathing zombie, but still, PAIN

You CANNOT escape, you CANNOT hide; you *must* **COPE**
Just TAKE IT

They do not know your suffering, they CANNOT know, *will* not know

CUT YOU OPEN; add new parts; take some out; STILL PAIN, just **COPE**

"Doctors know all" They know NOTHING
"This one's the BEST" CANNOT help ME

Wants to keep me comfortably NUMB- I need my LIFE BACK

"We CANNOT make right what is now so wrong"

Wires in my spine, metal in my ribs, foreign in my body
Cold, stainless steel, steal; doesn't take away my PAIN

"These drugs will *help* you **COPE**"

NIGHTMARES, HALLUCINATIONS, INCOHERANT BABBLE
STUTTER, SLUR, A SHELL OF WHAT I ONCE WAS
THE LIVING DEAD, BUT THE DEAD FEEL NO *PAIN*

SHIVER, COLD SWEAT, ALL CONSUMING, FORGETFUL,
RESENTFUL, DEPRESSED, BITTER, HELPLESS; **DOPE**

HIGH AS A KITE, PAIN FREE FOR TWO HOURS

SLEEP, THE ONLY ESCAPE, EXCEPT DEATH- (NOT AN OPTION)

Wake UP; Pray for **Strength,** to face the **"NEW"** day

When will this end**? PAIN FOR LIFE**

Move slowly, take your time**; learn *how* to COPE**

KEEP THE FAITH, YOUR ONLY CHOICE
    His suffering was so much more
Someday this will end....HOPE

THE TRACKS

She's at the track, her boy at side, with her baby in her arms
She's waiting for the train you see, for husband and his charms

The forest gloom surrounds them deep
The tracks are empty, a close pack creeps

Dusk on its foreboding way
She shows no fear, her strength won't sway

The message that she won't receive
The train broke down, it did not leave

She'll wait too long, "some trains run late"
She does not know, she's sealed her fate

The wolves back off, the tribe moves in
Men took their land, blame all white skin

She'll not perceive them, but feels the blow
The children were spared, she'll never know

Her body lies so still and cold
The children into slavery sold

Time has passed, tracks now hide deep
Blood long ago into earth did seep

Bones and soil, all now one
Tall plants grow from her life now done…

She stands here now, babe and boy at side
She waits at dusk, and fear must hide

The train's arrival, for her, no, never
Like a photo, alone forever

WAITING TO DIE
FOR DAD, FROM MOM

For some the task is frightening, they know not where they'll be.
For David time passed slowly, his trusting heart could see.

David knew what to expect, it was his lifelong goal.
His faith had taught him early on, that Jesus held his soul.

Cancer wracked his body, but his soul was still secure.
Dave spoke with Jesus daily; his words were strong and sure.

The Bible was his text book. His heart opened his mind.
His eyes saw God around him, sweet mercies of every kind.

Dave saw only good in others, he never saw them stained.
By seeing love and kindness, he had everything to gain.

Jesus waits with open arms; Dave keeps his eyes on Him.
His Savior made the sacrifice, and David has no sin.

For when I hear the praises start,
    I want to rain upon you.
Blessings that will fill your heart,
    I see no stain upon you.
Because you are my child, and you know me.

      Keith Green, "When I Hear the Praises Start"

MY LOVE

Though darkness plagues you, I can see your light
'Tis to visualize rage, when you're in my site

Your presence so heavy, your resistance is power
But your heart shines so brightly, at the darkest of hours

As your muscles tense, pent up with such anger
I'm drawn helplessly, though such a dark stranger

Your eyes a dark brown, like your long, raven hair
My eyes held in captive, an endless blank stare

When you first took me into steely, strong arms,
My heart reached for yours, and awoke hidden charms

Alone, am I allowed to witness
That softer side, past stone; skins thickness

You've had nine lives, a dangerous past
Now for my soul's worth, our love does last

How quickly does your kindness hide
When the world awakens your more "honest" side

If only through my eyes you'd see,
What every heart could surely be

For now the anger, does quickly surface
Our opposite poles, my love's sole purpose

The Yin and Yang, the light and dark,
One cannot succeed, without the other's mark

Our hearts are joined, with magnetic force
The Lord's own plan, our love's true source

Without dark surroundings, our light would be dim
But our love's own survival, depends solely on Him

The pull is so strong, negative, positive together
But out in the world, enemies wish to break tether

The world as you see it; so ruined, so lost
My heart longs to save it, no matter the cost

I cannot deny the passion you stir
Unleash your fury, my thoughts are a blur

As your eyes soften, your muscles relax,
I see all your goodness, through your chosen mask

The mask that protects you, keeps you from harm
But often restricts you, from His loving arms

If only you knew, God the way that I do
Your light would flood out, black fading to blue

Those whom you loathe, and can't stand the sight,
See them through my eyes and find suppressed light

Your heart is afraid, fear makes you so pensive
When others approach, jump to defensive

To see their good, you find no just cause
Your judgment follows, when they break *your* laws

"This one's too lazy, to me, she is worthless"
But we cannot know, what lies beneath the surface

Her heart is broken, her love was lost
Her life's lost meaning, her burden's dark cost

We cannot know, what hardships have past
To make her listless, pointlessness last

Of coarse we all have many flaws,
But another can't dig, to find the cause

It's not for us to judge one's life
Self examination's needed, to dull our sharp knife

Let the Lord decide, each soul's fate
Their worthiness, not for *us* to rate

If we walked in their scarred, torn, shoes,
We'd find in the end, we, our prejudice, lose

Your emotion's passion, 'tis my elation
Our time together, a selfish vacation

But there is love, beyond our doors
All God's children, witness the scores

'Tis true, many have lost their way
Where their souls are destined, not for us to say

So, cloud your vision, from all their faults
Let your heart breath, unseal the vault

Raise no fist, and smash no door
Their redemption lies in so much more

Be patient with them, as I hope He will be,
When I reach Heaven's gate and God judges me

I'll hold you close, my breast your protection,
From the world's suffering, and your own reflection

Now hold me love, we're the lucky ones
Given new life, from the only Son

For your fire burns with such intensity, I am drawn like a moth to a flame
But with the Lord's light inside of me, your heart does much the same

MARISSA

Immediately, as I enter the door
Her presence bold, as a lions roar

Comes down the stairs to examine me
She soon realizes, that I too, can see

Sitting there, rag doll in tow
Closer now, what do I know?

Her past flashes before my eyes
Her parent's death, her Uncle's lies

Her room it would become her coffin
Aunt by marriage, would visit often

Her closet becomes her sanctuary
When fever arrives, life seems so scary

Aunt is beaten, but girl's forgotten
Her long blue dress, of pinafore cotton

When illness envelopes, she's allowed no doctor
So in her room, her Uncle locked her

He never wanted, a father to be
How dare he be asked to cater to she?

"She'll be fine, don't waste my time"
Alone she sleeps, Aunt sees the signs

Tried to sneak, find a way to heal
But Uncle discovered, her fate was sealed

She'll hold her doll, so scared and alone
An Uncle who hates, love can't condone

When Death, he came, to hold her at last
No tears or regret, when Uncle's eyes cast

Now he is doomed, but she has the sight
But neither on time, walked into the light

But here I am, to set her free
His cigars I smell, but cannot see

I shall sit and succumb to the trance
Into her sweet heart, my soul will glance

"How I miss my mom and dad"
"But I'm so afraid" her heart, so sad

"These two little girls, they are my friends"
"But when they grow up, the fun will end"

"The light welcomes you, your parents, they wait"
"Your time is at hand, you mustn't hesitate"

The young living girl, here in this household,
Has played and sung with her lost soul

But now it's time to say goodbye,
And end her suffering, it's OK to cry

Now as the girl, prepares to leave
A loving touch, the living receive

She's been here more than ninety years
Her soul released, with loving tears

But as for him, no "better place"
His own cruelty, he soon will taste

REMOVING THE LOG IN YOUR EYE

Everything is hidden in plain site
All you have to do is open your eyes

Open your heart, open your ears
Just stop being distracted by your own selfish needs

This appears to be a difficult task
Even true compassion centers on improving oneself

It is a rock and a hard place
We are blinded by self mutilation

Only to find the answer was in front of your eyes
From the beginning

BY FAITH

HEBREWS 11: 1
    Now faith is being sure of what we hope for and certain of what we do not see.

HEBREWS 11: 3
    By faith we understand that the universe was formed at God's command, so that what is seen was not made out of what was visible.

HEBREWS 11:4b
    ...By faith he was commended as a righteous man, when God spoke well of his offerings. And by faith he still speaks, even though he is dead.

HEBREWS 11: 6

And without faith it is impossible to please God, because anyone who comes to Him must believe that He exists and that He rewards those who earnestly seek Him.

HEBREWS 11: 7

By faith Noah, when warned about things not yet seen, in holy fear built an ark to save his family. By his faith he condemned the world and became the heir of righteousness that comes by faith.

Referenced from: Pocket thin New Testament with psalms & proverbs
New/international/version
Zondervan Publishing House
Grand Rapids, Michigan
Copyright 1973, 1978, 1984 by International Version

WAKE UP LITTLE GIRL

The alarm goes off just one more time
Nauseates me to hear its chime

Now I've only half an hour
To eat my breakfast, dress, and shower

Why do I need to sleep so much?
So still and heavy, beds soft touch

Need to escape, from all that's real
Fantastic journeys, with eyelid's seal

So soft my step, past lives explored
Souls and homes, walk through the door

Forest dark, rivers fast and deep
Through my minds eye, subconscious creep

This dreamlike state, seems far more real,
Than my conscious life, could ever feel

I walk into a room so dark
All lights black out, with one sharp spark

Ghosts speak to me, once walked the Earth
Centuries before my own stark birth

They show their love, they show their fears
They speak strange words, face soaked with tears

But once awake, I long to be
Back in the haze, where visions see

This life seems void, not quite complete
With depth of dreams, it can't compete

The substance such, it's like a drug
Drapes present simplicity, like a rug

In REM I walk, in queenly state
With far more worth, than this life rates

Sometimes visions, sometimes truth
Sometimes meaning stays aloof

Sometimes future, sometimes past
If only the memory is here to last

All dream the future- you do too
You remember these visions, as Déjà vu

GHOST TOWN

This ghostly city, so dark and gray
Even on the brightest day

To me, all I see is haunting gloom
The sadness, cries, of souls in doom

Shadow filled windows, to me, so much more
This city's wound bleeds like an open sore

Few of you witness, that which I do
My helplessness in this light, I rue

Reaching arms, faces and masks
Need spiritual throngs to complete the task

As I drive by, both day and night
My heart just breaks, at this lost sight

Some took their own life, some another's
Some just confused, hide and take cover

I cannot offer them more than prayer
Too much for me, I start not to care

Each soul is longing, for one just to hear
Our craft too monstrous, to me it's so clear

Feeling their woes, enduring their sorrow
Can't help you today, but maybe tomorrow

THE FORBIDDEN FRUIT

From "the beginning", but still around
In all kinds of "jungles", it can be found
In our labs, and on the ground

It opens your eyes, but please be wary
So easily found, sought not too rarely
Once true face shown, quite hopeless and scary

Do you control it, or does it cause you to drool
Open your eyes, you're playing the fool
Addiction takes charge, your life it will rule

Artists and medicine men see the sights
But terror comes quickly, in harsh, hectic nights
Vision and wisdom turns readily to fright

Just one taste can do the trick
Needle, swallow, snort, or lick
Wisdom fades and makes you sick

ALWAYS WANT WHAT YOU CANNOT HAVE

You always crave, what you cannot obtain
Never satisfied, drive yourself insane

What I've been given, I know comes from Him
To reject content happiness; such a foolish sin

Lust and greed, overpower your being
God given worth, I believe without seeing

Torture yourself with cravings relentless
Masochism involuntary, to me seems so senseless

The ultimate pride, the ultimate prize
Now hold in your hand, wanted once with your eyes

How quickly you tire of what's now your possession
Eyes look past treasure, to heart's next obsession

Grass looks so green, where your feet ne're do tread
Thirst never quenched, once you've lost to your head

Take a small taste, observe your reaction
Now fill your mouth, such fleeting satisfaction

"It's not the catch, but the thrill of the chase"
Your existence is lacking, your life such a waste

Happiness always there for the taking
But with covetous nature, your own life forsaking

Your wife is so beautiful; so loving, so kind
But his wife's says "no", now you're tunnel blind

If she said "yes", another you'd seek
You corrupt your own soul, the decay of it reeks

Once life passed you by, and you're in your dark tomb
Heaven's just out of reach, an eternity of gloom

HOW WE LIMIT OUR OWN SITE

Distract ourselves with the tangible

Things we can grasp, figures and "facts"

Touch with our hands, see with our eyes

How hopeless to hold onto material things, so fleeting

And so useless, without the soul, so eternal

Droning on, day after day

Occupying ourselves with toys, entertainment, money, sex

There is no point, if there is no soul

Make the most of this life! Why, if it is not a learning experience to perfect our being?

Pointless

We cannot love ourselves, if we cannot love each other, if we cannot love, period

How tedious to think love is a chemical imbalance, our hormones reacting to a physical stimulus

Do we not feel? Do we not lose control of our emotions from time to time? Is our permanent love, not permanent?

If the "bad" things in life did not happen, how would we define "good"?

If there is no eventual outcome for the soul, what is there to live for?

Dwell on worries, monetary loss or gain, toil on and on, then die

There is so much more to be gained, so much more to learn

Why do you limit yourselves so? You want to know where the Universe ends, but refuse to believe in creation.

I pity you for your blindness. You have gauged out your own site.

Emptiness, shallowness, we are given so much, yet limit ourselves to the obvious.

The obvious is a mere deception of what we perceive as "reality"
It confuses us, makes us ignorant to a deeper understanding of what is real.

Time is limited only to our perception of it, there is no law of physics that says it cannot move backwards, just ask Albert Einstein.

Are the stars that are light years away already dead, or are we?

THE RETURN

An eerie silence fills the air
Birds and mammals stop and stare

The heaven's full, a ghastly glow
And now begins the Holy show

The sky is black, now as the sun
This unique eclipse, *It* has begun

The traitor sky, with sun and moon
This bloody mask, escort of doom

The clouds grow thick, to blanket sky
Hurricanes circle, the deceptive eye

Lightning striking, death and fire
Prophets foretold of this future, dire

Destruction and mayhem, on Earth's every corner
The final Trumpet, all humans will mourn her

The Lord arrives, now as a Sword
He cuts them down, evil thrives no more

Graves crack open, fire rockets down
Lava flows, splits open ground

The burning flesh, mercy no more
Rise living dead, and flesh is torn

And as the skin begins to peal
Each layer of doubt, it will reveal

No death will come to subdue pain
Searing burns and slicing rain

No place to run, nowhere to hide
Remorse and tears, Relinquished Bride

Some souls will get a second chance
They'll suffer too, but some can last

Now the smoke and ash the air
Choking, burning, flesh and hair

The graves are open, the dead will walk
All nightmares real and demons stalk

Now on Earth begins his reign
Satan rules those who will remain

The Lord has shown, the truth to be
Knowing now, what sins we see

Forever separate, now from God
A torture worse than whip or rod

To know *you* chose, this fate *you* made
Did not accept the price HE paid

It's now too late, in darkness suffer
So alone, in fire and sulfur

No relief for an eternity
How to keep your sanity

He crept in like a thief at night
But t'was foretold, witnessed this sight

What had you done, this Hell to get
Once knew His Son, but did forget

Once a priest, but then denied
Knew the truth, now trust the lies

How could you chose, to reject His Son…
After God's own Love was sent, you're DONE

For those who didn't have the time,
To see the truth, they will survive

To toil and hide, under Satan's thumb
But sacrifice for the Chosen One

Keep the faith; it's your last chance
Upon the Sword, your eyes did glance

You know His power, have seen the light
But WE believed, without proof's sight

Now as the Bride, feast at the table
Praising, peace, free and able

We'll pray for you, as you bleed
Avoiding death and Satan's seed

And when our Lord, decides your fate,
We hope to join you, at Heaven's gate

But when the final curtain falls,
Satan's rule ends, breaks down the wall

All evil, souls, and demons die
Lucifer rots, now ends the lie

The Earth reborn, we now return
In Paradise, with the rest who've learned

THE BRIDEGROOM

They say it is better to have loved and lost, but can this be the truth?
With pain that aches down through your soul, a pain that kills your youth

You cannot prove it, or put it in verse
You cannot quell it, like you would your thirst

The one who has not loved at all,
Knows not the strength of yearning's call

To meet the one who completes your being
Two hearts as one; knowing, beating

Ripped away by fate's vast claws
Not just or fair, did we break His laws?

The sin had yet to be completed
Forgiveness given, as we needed

His healing from above; just seems so far
But our hearts and salvation help heal His scar

Our earthly love, seemed so intense
Obsessive lust, conquered all sense

We were not worthy of something so real
Taking truth's place, as He could feel

For kisses and embraces, I'll remain most grateful
For some are wanting and their hearts are hateful

Blessed be the lonely, unrequited, and poor
He'll give His love freely, if they knock at His door

Lord witness our pain, and forgive our weak trust
For we know you'll be back, and for our sake you must!

His earthly pain not to be equated, increased when they stop believing
Our sadness, self pity all aside, sacrifice leads to glory receiving

MORNING PRAYER

For a fresh start, I ask each day
Lying awake, alone, I pray

My eyes are dry, my heart is numb
Your kingdom, my Lord; I'll wait, please come

An eternity for us, for You, but a moment
My heart strains to cleanse, as I lie in my torment

Each moment that passes, another soul fails
Am I now so "lukewarm", not to care, tell Your tales?

NO! When I cry, I rejoice and I sing
But no one here wants to wait for a king

So, I'll remain, stay a sheep in wolves clothing
I will wait for their howls as they face their last warning

Then, I'll dust off my sandals, and I'll take Your hand
When You take me home, leave the suffering and damned

My eyes are dry
My faith is old
My heart is hard
My prayers are cold
    Keith Green, "My Eyes Are Dry"

MY GREEN EYE'S TURNIN' BLACK

Watch me change into a ghost
Soon to meet the Heavenly Host

Pain killers glorified, said to heal
Only true self, do they reveal

The agony still remains the same
Addiction's driving me insane

Pain so real, will last forever…
So, part of my body, they now sever

Surgery; now my pain is worse
Must I continue to suffer this curse?

Now they will, increase the dose
Watch me change into a ghost

PIOUS

Eyes upon me, as I rise above them
To the alter; pride, confidence summon

They are beneath me, feel my might for free
To talk to God, they MUST speak through me

"*I* will send your prayers to Him"
"12 'Hail Mary's' to release your sin"

I have the power, watch as I stride
While my dark secrets, I'm able to hide

Kiss my ring and fill my pockets
Wear His death, as I would a locket

Recreate the vision, of brutality and torture
Their guilt weighs heavy, for "tithe" to ensure

Memorized penance, as judgment is passed
Hypocritical, all my hidden acts

Make up *our* rules, as century passes
Distort the word, and slaughter the masses

Inquisitions and conquests, justified by *the* cause
All to our benefit, as we create new laws

What does *faith* have to do with my reign?
My hidden acts, if found out; quite insane

You worship Him, you worship me
Blind to my deception, but someday will see

Not all of us are deceptive and cruel
But we love the power that brought us to rule

You are not welcome, among *our* strict kind
Believe in Christ, but no rosary to find

Get out of this church, stand behind our tall wall
How *dare* you **expect,** a welcome for all?

Your belief's not enough to pass through our doors
My self righteousness; my pride's oozing sore

Rosaries and memorized prayers
Secret lust and wanton stares

Stained glass, stained gold; steeple so high
All others are wrong, their faith is a lie

Vow of poverty for you, but here kiss my ring
What's good for you, is my praises to sing

My robes and my hat, make me alright to trust
Now tell me your secrets, my knife I will thrust

Bow down before me, I am your superior
Your vessel to God, your soul is inferior

My Reign is temporary, I know deep in my soul
For now I'm above them, my pride takes its role

When at last, final judgment is here
I shall witness the truth; God's vengeance, my fear

NOTHING VENTURED, NOTHING GAINED

The box is made of porcelain and steel
So carefully designed, to hide what you feel
Rarely does it open your heart to reveal

How carefully and painstakingly constructed
"Inflict pain, 'fore you're hurt", it's instructed
A ticking bomb; and so easily destructed

To share your heart, trust in her- just so gullible
She seems nice, she seems sweet, appears so loveable
But don't take that chance, open up, don't be vulnerable

The risk is too high, no matter the gain
Just not a possibility, that she feels the same
Count on the years; count the sand and its grains

All this time, save your pride, build your heart out of stone
Spend your time with yourself, how you feel so alone
Life's true love, comes and goes, in your heart, finds no home

I, as a boy, I believed the saying, the cure for pain is love
How would it be, if you could see the world from my eyes?

Supertramp, "Hide In Your Shell"

CALL US SLAVES/2 CORINTHIANS 6:1-10

Call us slaves, sheep to the slaughter
Say what you will, I'll remain His daughter

Who is the predator, who is the prey?
You follow *your* "leaders", believe all they say

Blind leading blind, to death incomprehensible
To believe what's not seen, "no, that's not sensible"

WITHOUT THE SOUL, WITHOUT SALVATION, WHAT IS YOUR LIFE WORTH?

2 CORINTHIANS 6:1-10

As God's fellow workers we urge you not to receive God's grace in vain. For He says,

"In the time of my favor I heard you, and in the day of salvation I helped you."

I tell you, now is the time of God's favor, now is the day of salvation.

We put no stumbling block in anyone's path, so that our ministry will not be discredited. Rather, as servants of God we commend ourselves in every way: in great endurance; in troubles, hardships and distresses;

in beatings, imprisonments and riots; in hard work, sleepless nights and hunger; in purity, understanding, patience and kindness; in the Holy Spirit and in sincere love; in truthful speech and in the power of God; with weapons of righteousness in the right hand and in the left; through glory and dishonor, bad report and good report; genuine, yet regarded as imposters; known, yet regarded as unknown; dying, and yet we live on; beaten, and yet not killed; sorrowful, yet always rejoicing; poor, yet making many rich; having nothing, and yet possessing everything.

AMEN BROTHER!

Referenced from: Pocket thin New Testament with psalms & proverbs
New/international/version
Zondervan Publishing House
Grand Rapids, Michigan
Copyright 1973, 1978, 1984 by International Version

THE DEMON

Invisibility and a changeling soul, hides in our thoughts anonymously

Preying on our curiosity

Whispers hot temptations to our prideful, lustful, hidden selves

Doesn't care how many souls he uses for his own pleasures, when so many are willing

Hallucinations of our own wanted treasures

Grasping fingers of desire, reaching for unseen fire

You're gonna get burned

See his superficial beauty, how he shines for our amusement

True face can only be witnessed through purity's eyes

How easily we take his hand, how readily heed his command

So many places at one time, so many lives to undermine

Inspiration, judgment, advantage, pride; no one can ever completely hide

He knows our darkest feelings and fears; insecure and defensive, our inferior tears

So easy to follow his deceitful lead, his power our weakness, he often succeeds

So what is our only defense? To find our life's true happiness

WE WANT WHAT WE CANNOT HAVE, TO
BE SATISFIED WITH WHAT WE ARE GIVEN
FROM ABOVE BRINGS TRUE HAPPINESS

WE OURSELVES ARE TO BLAME

THE PASSENGERS

We've taken this route, so many times
No need to glance at the passing signs

Our friendship grandfathered, our car filled with laughter
Out playing pool, and a nice dinner after

Driving so fast, it feels like we're soarin'
Suddenly the road and the town seem so foreign

The sun has long set, it's way after midnight
The atmosphere thickens, it just doesn't feel right

Now, there's no street lamps, just unending field
An abyss of infinity, road through my windshield

I start to slow down, for the fear's creeping in
My friends got the map out, can't read in this din

My heart starts to race, as I speak in third person
My friend's in a panic, "we must go!" she is cursing

I now feel their presence, the car they're surrounding
I step on the gas, we're flying, we're bounding!

It's a tribe full of demons, now swarming the car
Have to look straight ahead, impulse fights me hard

I see in my mind's eye, his menacing face
Must get to their boundary, we are now in a race

With his piercing eyes, bald but for the Mohawk
All loyal to him, joined as one, kill and stalk

If I grow weak, and turn just a stitch
Our eyes will make contact, end up in a ditch

What have we done, to deserve this attack?
In my rear mirror, two new guests in the back

In their own time, they had become prisoners
This tribe raped and butchered, evilest of sinners

The Great Spirit's decided, purgatory no more
Success; past their border, my foot on the floor

Is it the speed, or all in our head?
The car raises up, a feather of lead

These new passengers, from a time long ago
A couple forbidden, love ever to show

She a white maiden, with long, silken hair
He, Native American, all spoke with his stare

My living friend, can't see them per se
But describes from her head, what they wore on that day

We are almost there, I must concentrate
He wants me to fail, has plotted our fate

But their "Great Spirit", is our "Great God"
He'll deal with them soon, with benevolent rod

He'll see us through safely, we will complete task
And to sing Him sweet praises, is all that He asks

We've done it; we're safe, no further they'll go!
Back to their own Hell, glad to miss that freak show

Now safe to stop, evaluate circumstances
And now in strange tongue, I hear and see dances

To convert into words, overwhelming gratitude
With my heart, hear his thanks, reaching highest latitude

Joined forever in love, with excitement they're reeling
Singing God's praises, dancing and kneeling

My heart is so glad, with our task now completed
Look up to see sign, know right where the car's seated

With heartfelt tears, together rejoicing
All praise the Great Spirit, a mercy worth voicing!

VIOLENCE AS AN APHRODISIAC

Watch him and his pent up rage
A weaker man, just can't engage

Every movement meaningful
Without him even knowing so

I crave his presence, know he's mine
Feared by some, no just cause why

He'd never hurt me, just shows love
Sometimes handled with kid glove

Exterior, so sharp and fierce
With his eyes, a soul can pierce

Muscles tight, fists are clenched
With cold sweat, my body's drenched

Like iron and steel, his truth and mind
His heart did soften, with love, so kind

Drawn to darkness, but led by the light
When his heart joined mine, all Heaven's delight

Cannot describe it, cannot explain
Why the bad boy, my heart did claim

All stored up darkness, exchanged into light
To be joined together, just know, is so right

Nothing more flattering, or so real
Than a once broken heart, my love did heal

Thank you Lord, for we are so blessed
I never had known, genuine happiness

A SHADOW IN THE DARK

Why don't you come to me?
I may just set you free
Or would you choose to be
Here for an eternity

My heart does mourn for you
See my eyes, and know it's true
Do all that I can do
With prayer, it's just we two

For us the Lord did bleed
And now you feel the need
For you I beg and plead
To save your soul indeed

Our hearts can join as one
And soon you'll meet the Son
I weep for the deeds you've done
Your eternity's already begun

Love and light to show the way
Alternative, here forever stay
Now on knees we both will pray
Forgiveness comes today

I am a stranger to you
Yet my words are all too true
Your heart is black and blue
You grieve to start anew

Like a snake, you'll shed your skin
And with it all your sin
Please let us come to Him
Love, hope, and peace begin

Dark shadows cannot hide
How much you ache inside
He healed and never lied
Let us walk to the other side

Please use this vessel here
I'll hurt and shed your tears
You've suffered all these years
As a victim of your fears

THE CHIEF

When you saw me first, I was a child
Didn't show yourself, you simply smiled

You didn't need me, from beyond your grave,
For all this land, to you, He gave

And in your heart you always knew,
Your Heaven here, my heaven to

I can only come here twice a year
But when I leave, I shed some tears

Its beauty for me, is unsurpassed
Old growth trees, survived logging past

First time we met, off the trail and lost
But only by twenty feet we crossed

"Silly women", understood you to say
"So close to the trail, yet can't find your way"

You gathered your strength from surrounding forest
In full chiefly garb, even headdress for us

Back to our trail, you led the way
And "Come back again", I felt you to say

You have your borders, so far between
And all of your splendor, I've felt and seen

Every year, we manage to meet
With the certain smell of history, you greet

An old familiar freshness it seems
And you visit deep within my dreams

But when I'm in your forest so grand,
Enveloped with reverence of this land

I share this feeling, as you well know
For every year our connection grows

You knew the Great Spirit, as leader and friend
Led with courage and wisdom, until the end

Once, while in the cabin I lay
I saw you there, as clear as day

This time long hair, but no headdress
Vivid true form, was your success

Just to let me know you're there
Because you know I need and care

In every leaf and every breeze,
I feel your presence, when I can't see

When I leave, my heart does break
Piece of this land, with me, I take

I will return and when I'm here,
We'll meet again, this time next year

THE SOULMATE

For the first time, my knees actually weak
Went to open my mouth, it was to dry to speak

His eyes a deep brown, his hair dark to match
All the lady's had said, "He's a definite catch"

I found that his beauty, had far surpassed mine
But through all my faults, he vowed *my* soul shined

Our passion engulfed us, with an intensified fire
But no touch was allowed, to quench our desires

Independently realized, that before we were born,
Our hearts knew each other, for an eternity sworn

But not in this lifetime, could a union be made
With a wife and his children, his marriage is saved

For our happiness to be, other hearts would be broken
Forced to deny love, so much pain left unspoken

He left with his family, and I remained here
Not able to hold me, no more could stand near

I know with all faith, someday it will be
Our souls reunited, in Heaven's vast sea

We made the right choice, our minds truly knew
With my wedded love, I'll forever stay true

THE FINAL CHOICE

In the darkness of the early morn,
Cries of anguish, souls lost and scorn

Hear them weep and gnash their teeth,
As Sword's true glory, is now unsheathed

The Lord returns not as a child,
But as the Truth, burns free and wild

For those who had not met Him yet,
Perhaps a second chance they'll get

But in misery, they will remain,
Now knowing God and Christ the same

Their life no longer as they knew it,
Suffering now, must struggle through it

For those who led a better life,
The Kingdom's feast and no more strife

He chose to wait, so He could see,
The weak in faith, that chose to flee

And those who knew and then rejected,
No second chance, worse Hell subjected

Their torture more than any other,
Knew the truth, but let world smother

To hide from those who "rule" this Earth,
From those who'd mock, so blind from birth

The choice was made, they sealed their fate,
And now realize, it's much too late

Fire and brimstone not enough,
Separation from God, is far more tough

He loved and cared and helped them through,
Yet they rejected, so sad, but true

Whom once were saved, but now are lost,
For a worldlier life, pay the highest cost

For those who knew and faith did keep,
Their faults forgiven, when bodies seep...

Into the ground, no longer needed,
Free at last, in Heaven greeted

No more pain, no struggling or fears,
Rejoicing many, with heartfelt tears

Our hearts still break for those behind,
Though they were so selfish and unkind

Some will get just one last chance,
It won't be easy, under Satan's lance

He'll make it your burden, through toils and snares,
To save your soul, the Cross you'll bear

But here today, choice is simply made,
Accept the Truth, Jesus already paid

He care's for us, He sends His love,
He gave His Life, guides from above

To accept the Truth, is all you need,
The smallest gesture, to Heaven speed

When the redemptive chance is up,
Those who persevered, shall drink the Cup

When Satan's rule comes to bitter end,
Hell too terrible, to describe my friend

And those who took the "wider path",
Shall perish too, in God's sworn wrath

Eternity in Hell's dark home,
So afraid, and so alone

And once again the Earth is made,
Into our Kingdom of gold and jade

Forever in beauty, forever in love,
Now with the Lord, no longer above

CHRISTIAN CHAOS

It is not comfort, it is not fine
To feel numb, is not sublime

I need to feel, I need the sting
The pain inside, to cry or sing

Emotion, chaos; on which I thrive
Without such things, I'd not survive

This world in which we all revolve
Needs the problems, we live to solve

It is my goal, my soul the same
To help the others through this game

The Lord has given much to me
From me expects, much more, you see

A life of comfort, free and clear
Leads my soul to ache with fear

Heaven on Earth, could not exist
Enjoy your time, but don't resist...

The things in Life that must be done
Before, the return of the living Son

On Earth so brief, not meant to last
Must make up for sins in our lives past

The issues found important here
So futile when the truth's made clear

For now, I'll wait for my next task
Mediocrity, shame's lifeless mask

Lord, reach me, I know there's more
With uselessness, my heart grows sore

THE LOGIC OF FAITH

What's that you say? By definition, faith defies logic. I beg to differ. Although, it is true, that those of us who believe do not need facts to prove our faith. We know it is as true as the love we feel in our hearts for those we are close to. It is something that cannot be charted, graphed or experimented on. Not mere hormones, adrenaline, or desire; but something deeper inside, something unconditional. Something that is felt just as strongly during the quiet moments together, as it is during the heat of passion. However, for those skeptics out there who require a more scientific approach, let me have a moment of your precious time to address some facts and theories I have discovered. They combine science, common sense, and faith itself. Yes, it is possible.

First, allow me to remind you that scientists have proved that most of us only use a small portion of our grey matter for cognitive thought. But, an exceptional man like Albert Einstein, DID NOT disprove the idea of a creator, either did Darwin. You may assume that, just because his discoveries are interpreted in a certain way in the world of logic. Evolution is a theory, just as creationism is a theory. I happen to believe in both. I do believe that we have adapted or "evolved" over the years as the Lord intended us to. But I also believe that as all creatures, including the single celled ones; we were created by a being greater than ourselves. I believe God created many different kinds of monkeys first to test the waters, and then he created us, in his image, but with many differences. It is His breath that makes us unique. We have a soul that continues on after our mortality has finished our confinement off. Wait, just hear me out! Can our intestinal bacteria prove if we exist or not? I have evaluated my theories as scientifically as I can. There is no law of physics that says time cannot move forward, backward, or slow down according to how we perceive it. Just ask someone who was in a car accident, how long the seconds lasted. Isn't it just possible that six days to God, may be thousands or millions of years each to us? I think eternity would be unbelievable long if He perceived time the way we do our days on Earth. Awfully convenient one might say, I admit I don't know all the answers, but do you? People who thought the world was round instead of flat were once considered quite insane. But I digress.

Let me ask you, do you believe in the internet? *I don't know,* one contraption able to be all over the world at once, storing people's ideas, perversions, beliefs, humor, good deeds and bad, just because we take the time to tell "it". And, you can just look this stuff up, anytime, anywhere, with this little "magic box" that doesn't even have wires!! You're kidding me! And this box has all my information, accounts, my life, can shut down my power and everything!!! Well, gee, you might as well believe in "Santa Clause"! And you say humans created this thing? Well I guess I'll just have to take you word for it, but it sounds a little religu, I mean "REDICULUS" to me. What'll they think of next? Creating life in a laboratory, creating elements, life saving devises, eyes for the blind, limbs for the lame, now that's *ridiculous!* Just plain crazy talk! But of course I know I sound crazy to you, because I believe in an invisible being that can do all the same things. We can't see to the ends of the UNIVERSE, but we are quite sure there is nothing there that we don't know about. Do we at least know if it's round or flat?

All right, try this one on for size; all major religions have pretty much the same basic principles. The rules and traditions change drastically between what humans consider to be right. But, basically they strive for relative harmony, good morals, taking care of one's soul after this life, and respecting a "Creator". One who uses other beings; humans, prophets, preachers, angels, spirits, saints, and other minor deities, to take care of the beings created; us. We just use different names for our "Creator". Perhaps this creation took place in a GIANT LAB called "the universe", in a GIANT BEAKER called "the Earth". Things like fire, water and other appropriate elements were used in this creation, and perhaps it took millions of years. Perhaps the "Creator" experimented first with smaller beings, played with dinosaurs as a child, and then perfected His skills until He could create a being similar to Himself. He would give these beings free will, since no one can appreciate love that is forced to happen. He would want His creation to choose to love Him. Now perhaps, He would communicate often with His creation until He realized it would mean more, for them to love Him without constant reassurance. After a while, He saw His people stopped believing in Him when He wasn't around, so He decided that He would give them one last chance and send down a piece of Himself in human form. That way, He could show us just how much He loved us, and experience for Himself the trials of being a human. But we are a fickle people, and we quickly lose interest and find out it's much more fun to serve ourselves than to serve a God we can't see. At some point, the Creator is going to grow tired of our selfishness, and He will decide to save those He can, and wipe the slate clean of the "Riffraff". "But if you're living like there is no God- you'd better be right!" So what do you think He's waiting for, I don't know, if I spent millions of years creating something, I don't think I'd be real eager to destroy it, would you? I think maybe He's waiting to give every non-believer as many chances as possible, maybe He's waiting for this book to come out, or maybe He's waiting for YOU!

Although I am a Born Again Christian, I believe it is the pride of humans that distorts, distracts, rapes, pillages, plunders, and forces people to do things against their will. "Gee, most Born Again Christians that I know, say that if I don't act like them I'm going to burn in Hell!" Well anyone who says that is not following the Teaching of Christ. We were given the power to heal, forgive, and love, but NOT to judge the Human Soul. That right belongs to God alone. Nowhere in the Bible does it say we earn the right to judge others; however it does say "judge not, lest thee be judged and by the same measure" (Matthew 7:1-6). That's pretty specific. Perhaps if we could all get past our own personal pride for a day, we really could have Heaven on Earth, and God wouldn't have to destroy His creation. Corrupt religious leaders who have twisted faith to their own greater good, have done more harm than any amount of good deeds could fix. In doing so they are violating the morals of the faith they are preaching; humility, poverty, and chastity. It is greater sin not to practice what you preach, than to have no faith at all. I feel God judges us each by taking our own upbringing, morals, and surroundings into consideration. What kind of torture did you suffer at the hands of some so-called "believer"? I personally have only benefitted from knowing the Lord, so I haven't had any doubt for most of my life. But, I realize there are a lot of evildoers in the world, who choose to serve their own needs and then blame the Lord- I pity them for the Hell they will have to face for their actions. Therefore, who am I to say who will go to Hell? That's for God to know and you to find out. Even if I was wrong in my beliefs, my life was happier for knowing Christ. He has cared for me when no one else could, and carried me through my toughest moments. Do I use my faith as a crutch? Hell ya, and I'm not ashamed to admit it!

Now, how does that work, One God in three parts? Isn't that a bit hypocritical? Well, in order to have any kind of faith, you have to believe in the concept of a soul. A soul that perhaps after learning its lifetime of lessons, and passing or failing in its temptation tests, can move onto some other level. Well the scientific "ghost hunters" of the world, are doing a pretty good job of proving that something exists beyond the grave. But, most souls they "capture" are in some kind of limbo, or torment, or have some kind of unfinished business. Where have all the "satisfied with life" people gone? Hmmmm, perhaps someplace we cannot see with the naked eye, and have not yet invented a machine that can see for us. My theory is this, God the Father is like our brain, Jesus the Son is like our body, and the Holy Spirit is like our soul. All make up one human, but all three are needed to survive.

Now, I believe in miracles, and I obviously believe that the Lord can write His words through the hands of His creation. I do not have a doubt in my mind; I've seen far too much proof and so-called coincidences in my lifetime for doubt. However, I cannot guarantee beyond a shadow of a doubt, that although the Bible harshly warns against it, that no one has omitted or changed things over the years to serve their own interests. But, I also realize that Jesus spoke in parables and lessons for us to interpret during our faith journey. So perhaps there are contradictions in the Bible, it doesn't mean we can't learn from them. I also do not think God wants us to have all the answers. If God proved His existence there would be no more faith, or true love. If you pay a hooker to say "I love you" are you going to believe her? If a man holds a gun to your head, are you going to say what he wants to save your own skin? Why then would God want to force our love, doesn't it mean so much more, that we trust and love without proof? As for me, I don't care if logic defies faith, I have all the proof I need in my heart and soul; and I thank God that my life is a happy, blessed one! I pity those who cannot quench their thirst, or see the good that is all around them. I have felt the power of the Holy Spirit for myself, not just in church or because my parents believe, but alone in the woods with God's glory and creations all around me. I will wait patiently for the Great Revealing, and I know that each time I am mocked for my faith; my eternal crown grows with more precious jewels. You just keep on thinking the world is flat. No skin off my back. I don't know everything. I don't need to. I TRUST completely.

Sincerely,
Christine Chaos

P.S. I don't write under an assumed name because I am embarrassed of my faith. Anyone who knows me, knows my beliefs and that I can see and sometimes speak to the dead. I remain anonymous to protect the broken hearts I write about, and the sanctuary of my marriage and my quiet private life.

ACTS 17:29-31

"Therefore, since we are God's offspring, we should not think that the divine being is like gold or silver or stone-an image made by man's design and skill. In the past God overlooked such ignorance, but now he commands all people everywhere to repent. For he has set a day when he will judge the world with justice by the man he has appointed. He has given proof of this to all men by raising him from the dead."

Referenced from: Pocket thin New Testament with psalms & proverbs
New/international/version
Zondervan Publishing House
Grand Rapids, Michigan
Copyright 1973, 1978, 1984 by International Version